This Book Belongs To

[illegible]

[illegible]

Made in the USA
Monee, IL
09 December 2021

84526081R00063